Lilac and Sawdust

Lilac and Sawdust

poems

Kenneth Pobo

Emporia, Kansas, USA

Meadowlark Press, LLC
meadowlark-books.com
P.O. Box 333, Emporia, KS 66801

Lilac and Sawdust
Copyright © Kenneth Pobo, 2021

Cover Image:
"lilacs" by Muffet (https://www.flickr.com/photos/calliope/) is licensed under CC BY 2.0 To view a copy of this license, visit https://creativecommons.org/licenses/by/2.0/

Cover and Interior Design: TMS, Meadowlark Press

All rights reserved. This book or any portion thereof may not be reproduced or used in any manner whatsoever without the express written permission of the author except for the use of brief quotations in a book review.

POETRY / LGBT
POETRY / Subjects & Themes / Love
POETRY / American / General

Library of Congress Control Number: 2021946209

ISBN: 978-1-956578-00-3

For Stan

Lilac and Sawdust

Breakable

Jeff and Jerry Were Older ········· 3
Migrations ········· 4
Jeff & Jerry & the Everyday ········· 5
Cabinets ········· 6
Jeff and Jerry Wake Up One Saturday ········· 7
Jeff Sees His Old Church Is A CVS ········· 8
Jeff Knew ········· 9
Jerry Knew ········· 10
Brown Cords ········· 11
Page 234 ········· 12
Jerry and Maxine ········· 13
When Jeff Came Out ········· 14
Jerry Sings In The Attic ········· 15
Hose ········· 15
Jerry's Life As Sung To "I Think
    We're Alone Now" ········· 17
Jerry Coming Out To Mom Twice ········· 19
Breakable ········· 20

Rings in a Garden

Rings ········· 23
Door Locked ········· 24
Jerry Home ········· 25
Gunfire Buddha ········· 26
Jerry Says ········· 27
Jeff and Jerry on Separate Vacations ········· 28
Jeff and Jerry with the Travel Agent ········· 29
Jerry and Jeff in Cape May ········· 30
Jerry and Jeff at the International
    Peace Garden ········· 31
Missing Each Other ········· 32

Jeff, Jerry, & the Lap ··· 33
Caps ·· 34
Jerry Listening to the Wind ··································· 35
Mosquito Jeff ·· 36
Jeff and Jerry have Ants ··· 37
In Jerry's Dream ··· 38
Block Party ·· 39
Don't Talk (Put Your Head on My Shoulder) ······· 43
Indoor Garden ··· 44
Stung ·· 45
Magic ·· 46

Rituals

Evening Ritual ··· 49
Slobs ·· 50
Jerry's Luck ·· 51
Wood Blocks ··· 52
The First Fallen Petal ··· 53
Jerry says that being ··· 54
Cardboard Jeff ·· 55
Jerry Puzzles ·· 56
Jeff's Curtains ·· 57
Jerry Bats ·· 58
Jerry Grew Up Thinking ·· 59
Charley Pride Sings ··· 60
Robber ·· 61
Cracked Windowbox ··· 62
Jerry and Jeff Up ·· 63
Jerry and Jeff don't believe in ····························· 64
10:45 PM ·· 65

About the Author ··· 67
Publication Notes ·· 69

Jeff and Jerry Were Older

in their forties when they met.
The creek had widened
like their bellies. Time
felt a bit shorter,
a bit faster. Sex
was like falling into a hammock
after mowing the lawn, lulling
and pleasant. They had little
in common, though a bluebird's
blue returning in April
drew them both to the window.

They never go to clubs,
hardly go out to eat,
the *Everybody Loves Raymond* marathon
too tempting. The propane heater's
soft blue flicker
warms the room. Legs touch.

Night like a porch with a light
suddenly turned on.

Migrations

Before Jerry met Jeff, he had decided that love
was a coat rack and he had no coat.
Jeff had stacked up his affairs like dirty plates,

a fairly messy life. They met in a line
at Wal-Mart. In that rocky first year,
they argued about cabinets.
Jerry wanted open spaces, nothing stacked.
Jeff rarely threw anything away. The dining room
table grew heaps of newspapers. Once Jerry tried
to toss them out, but Jeff snarled,
"I was saving those for the sports sections!"
"The games are over. Try reading Twain instead."

They love birds. Jeff watches them on the shore
or flying when he goes fishing. Jerry never fishes.
He stays in the cabin with the binoculars
watching loons dart underwater.
Jeff gets up by 4:30 to catch the first nibbles.
When Jerry wakes up, he finds
the coffee already made,

Melitta coffee. A low-burning fire. A plate mountain
in the sink. You can't have everything.
You drink the coffee, see the boat
through the binoculars, and drift like a ripple.

Jeff & Jerry & the Everyday

You live in a house with a mailbox
snug against the road. Your gay
agenda: buying lightweight cat litter
and lightweight music. You both know
every lyric on the *Bubblegum Hits* CD.

Once upon a time someone slammed
your mailbox, left a threatening note.
Twice upon a time someone egged
your house. You're watched.
You see nothing from the window.
Sometimes. That lesbian couple
you met at the Unitarian church pot luck,
you remember when Marta told a story
about their cat getting stuffed
in the trash can. You're glad
your cats, Fred and Ethel, stay indoors.
Soon maybe you won't go outdoors.

You wait.
You watch.
It doesn't
stop.

Cabinets

As a toddler, Jeff would open all the kitchen cabinets by the floor. Sometimes he'd nap in one of them, head between a pot and a pan. Thirty years later he remembers how safe he felt once he had pulled the cabinet closed. He gave his mother

several frights when she'd call without getting a response. He became too leggy to fit in any cabinet. Ever since, he's been looking for a safe place. Even when he pulls the front door shut, closes the window blinds, and it's just him and Jerry and the cats, something feels off.

It's not so much that he fears a break-in, a thief hiding in the evergreens waiting for the lights to go out. It's a vague unease. His friend Irma feels unease when the power goes out during a thunderstorm, fears that the lights will never return. They always do—but she's a wreck.

Jerry watches when Jeff starts tapping his fingers on the side of the couch or begins to pace. "What's wrong?" "Nothing." He kisses the top of Jeff's head.

Night brings broken sleep. In the morning the sun car speeds down their street, narrowly misses the blooming magnolia tree. The cupboards would take him in if they could. A clattery opera of lids plays inside them. Jeff listens carefully. And tries to sing along.

Jeff and Jerry Wake Up One Saturday and Find Spray Painted on their White Garage Door FAGGOTS, Well, It Means FAGGOTS, but It's Spelled FAGOTS

Any number of people could have
done it. A nice neighborhood—
lawns dutifully mowed, no loud parties
even on weekends. Nice. And notes
stuffed in the mailbox that say
Were gonna get you. Perhaps
they will get them someday.

They've alerted
the police. Jerry remembers when he
was robbed years before he moved in
with Jeff, how the missing TV
ended up on a clipboard in the patrol car,
never even turned in. That's what
the secretary said at the station.

Help may come
or not. Either way, the garage
needs repainting. Tomorrow pops
up wearing torn fatigues.
The next message may be written
in blood.

Jeff Sees His Old Church Is a CVS

From age seven I sang in the choir.
Mrs. Selkie taught me
how to get notes to fall
just right. I got solos.

Deacon Pinter said he wished
every boy would be like me.
Maybe I didn't *look* gay—
he'd have kicked my ass
in a most unholy way,
as they all would. Long ago.

At work I make up tunes
I hum silently. A few I share
with Jerry who once egged me on
to audition for *Dancing With The Stars*.
I dance too. Today

The Bible Church of Tibbs Ford
is a drive-through CVS.
We get bagged drugs while eating
McDonald's fries. Pills,
a small blue choir in a bottle.
We swell with praise,
forget what we're praising.

Jeff Knew

Jeff worked hard on a book case
in seventh-grade Shop,
loved the lathe too much,
mis-shaped the wood.

Robert Finchetti,
just another kid with acne
and curly black hair—Jeff
knew staring was rude,
but wherever Robert went,
Jeff's eyes secretly followed.
He learned how to look
and not be caught—an art,
like building something
that wouldn't topple over.

Robert moved away.

Sometimes joy is The Sleeper
yo-yo trick, tough to learn—
It's in the spin. With practice
you get it, the yo-yo finding a way
back to your hand.

Jerry Knew

he was gay while eating Pez,
Joan Crawford in *Rain* on TV.
Newton had the apple
that showed him how to find a motel
named gravity. Jerry had Joan.

He was 18, knew at 13,
but knowing can be far from saying.

Yet he felt more sure
of the way, no map needed, love's
ostrich coming up

from behind, telling him to hop on.

Brown Cords

His first time in
a gay bar, Jeff wore
brown cords, a pack
of Newports in his pocket.
Some guy asked him to dance
to "Dancing Queen,"
put his hand on Jeff's ass—
part of him wanted to say
stop that,
part of him wanted to say
more please.

After the song ended,
the stranger slipped away
into other dancers.

Jeff ordered a gin and tonic,
more at ease
but ready to go.

Page 234

In books he read on the sly
at the library, the few that mentioned
homosexuality—except in a nasty
or stupid way—he learned that gay
men are distant from their fathers,
a great truth on page 234 in a book
written by a doctor.

Jeff enjoyed his dad, who played softball,
helped him with geometry problems,
watched reruns of *Rocky and Bullwinkle*.
What distance?

It took years for Jeff to take
a cigarette lighter and burn
the doctor's book, burn it right up,
every word. Not the real book,
he hadn't gone to that library in years,
but the one inside his head
where the doctor prescribed pills
made of lies, made him swallow.

Jerry and Maxine

Each Sunday, Jerry listens
to Mrs. Kessler talk about
the Apostle Paul's
fabulous journeys—he must
get to Rome. Jerry hopes
to someday lead an exciting
life like Paul's.
Killing people.
Seeing a light.

He names his favorite
paper doll Maxine.
She doesn't have to go
to school where
Mr. Dirmo calls him
a flaming
queer.

Maxine arrives
through the window
partly covered with
construction paper
valentines, takes Jerry
far away, to the moon
maybe, where root beer
floats have two straws,
Earth a napkin
fallen on the floor.

When Jeff Came Out

When Jeff came out
at seventeen, his Aunt Stokesia told
Pastor Blamp of the Oak Road Bible Church
who dashed over to the little yellow
ranch house behind big yellow dahlias
and shouted at Jeff, his fifty-two years
swinging at him like a mallet.
Jeff shut his eyes to stiff gray sideburns,
Blamp's voice a cranky leaf blower.
Blamp said he was all about love. Like God.
Didn't Jeff know that? Jeff
had wriggled free of Sunday suits.

Aunt Stokesia never spoke to Jeff again.
Died the following year, a bad heart.
Prayer, a fence she stayed behind.

Jerry Sings in the Attic

Jerry sings in the attic
among his grandfather's 1915 pencil sharpener,
boxes of Christmas decorations, suitcases,
and dishes they no longer use. Someday,
the garage sale. Downstairs, Jeff makes
cinnamon toast, the TV on loud,
Wheel of Fortune. A wheel spins,
letters pop up, and someone could
become a winner. This one day.
Jeff aches to polish off the puzzle.

Jerry escapes to the attic. The steps
creak behind a dark brown door that
he wishes were made of teakwood.
Too many things are dark in the house.
Once he's up there he can still hear
the TV, soft, like a couple of crickets.
He starts to sing: "Lovely Rita Meter Maid,"
"Lonesome Town," and "Hanky Panky."
He feels as if he's solved something—
off-key notes welcome him
as Grand Marshall to a parade.

Hose

Jerry fell in love for the first time
in college—Bill Ainsley,
a Mechanical Engineering major,
numbers his favorite garden. Strange
blossoms opened there.

Bill didn't want anyone to know.
Jerry wanted everyone to know.
They told no one.

Bill graduated and moved
to Louisville. Promises scorched
envelopes—love,
water dripping out of a hose
rolled up for winter,
the drops becoming fewer,
then none.

Jerry's Life as Sung to "I Think We're Alone Now"

Children behave. "Will you relax, Deanna, so what if the kid breaks a few things?" dad would say. Mom often looked like the last Kleenex in the box and no one was going to use her and throw her away. Her favorite expression: *Be on your toes.* I was on my toes, I suppose. Up for school. Hardly ever "sassy" when told to take out the garbage. When she died I learned that she had been on her toes for seventy-seven years. Her feet were damn tired. I never got her a pillow.

That's what they say when we're together. When I met Jeff, I had already come out to my parents. Jeff hadn't. He'd say, "They think that gay people are poison. We emit killing fumes." His family figured us out—we weren't "buddies." His mother remains cold but sends me Christmas cards with messages like "Remember Jesus's birthday. He remembers yours." His father thinks of me as another channel to change. I don't think they fear poison. Is this progress?

And watch how you play. I knew I was gay young. It's like I was a contestant on *You Bet Your Life* and the secret word, Gay, came down and yes, Groucho, that's me. I've felt watched all my life. I met my first lover, Ben, at Polk Junior High School. We could do anything we wanted provided we said "We're not gay. We don't love each other. Only gay people can love each other." That freed us to do what he called "the snooky ookums." Watched. By parents. Neighbors. School. I've spent decades dislodging eyes from my skin. Eyes in my most private places. *They don't understand.* Ben and I were "gross, weird, sinful, and only kooks do that kind of thing."

And so we're runnin' just as fast as we can. I ran and ran but they kept moving the finish line. After two and a half decades I realized that the finish line was in their heads, not mine. I stopped running. Even now, so many keep running, faster, faster—how do they do it? Bare feet. Gravel.

Holdin' on to one another's hand. Jeff's hand is my favorite part of his body. I don't rank his parts, but his hand is tops. When I hold it, deep blue forget-me-nots cover the most barren ground inside me. His hand is a map of wisdom. I don't read maps well, but I never feel lost as long as I have his hand.

Tryin' to get away into the night. My friend Mitch tried to get away for years. Booze, drugs, a bunch of guys he slathered all over his body. He quit trying. I was a pallbearer at his funeral. How easily it could have been me in the box. Mitch wore out from the daily battering ram of hate.

And then you put your arms around me and you say I think we're alone now. Alone is a rake standing by the garage door. It needs to be put to good use. Alone is sitting with Jeff watching *My Three Sons,* not saying anything, but knowing when he will laugh at Bub.

Alone is finding a place to hide, you think no one will ever find you, you're OK with that, kind of, but someone does find you. Hides with you. And emerges with you. Into light. And darkness.

Jerry Coming Out to Mom Twice

Mom wouldn't say "cancer."
We followed her lead. Dad said she was
"under the weather." I said she was
"feeling poorly." Opinions

hardened her spine. Her views were like math tests.
You got enough points and you passed.
Often I was the torn-up test,
the F in the ever-lengthening grade book.
Mom was the sound
of a loudly closed book.

She also couldn't say the word "gay."
I had "a problem." I was "different."
Not all that religious, God fell under
her math tests too. Even God could flunk.

Telling her that I worked as an environmentalist
freaked her out. "A what? I can see you
whistling on dark forest trails,
a bear swatting you down for good."
When I walk in the woods,
I don't whistle. My dreams are of bears,
deer, and snowbirds.

Mom always kept a clean house.
See boxes on the floor in mine.
Dusting? What? I want magic,

a forest that takes me in real deep.
No problem if I can't find my way back.

Breakable

Jerry and Jeff sit on the porch
watching fireflies bring light
without sound. It's their
twelfth anniversary.
They date it from when they
met at the flea market, an album bin,
fifty cents each. Candlelight
and wine, a conversation about

fish sticks. Their neighbor,
Alice Karshaw, comes outside
and bangs trash can lids together.
Jeff says, "Ignore her!"
Jerry says, "Maybe I can calm her."
That never works. Last fall
he started a chat with her—
she demanded that he shovel up
dust that blows from their lawn
onto hers. Jerry pretended to do it.
Jeff: *she's a radio station—tune her out.*

The trash-can symphony swells
as Jerry yells "Knock it off!"
The guys hear her crying beyond
the apple tree. Her door slams.
Lights out. They sit in silence

like houseplants, rise to bring in
gold-rimmed glasses,
the most breakable ones.

Rings in a Garden

Rings

Jeff and Jerry get wedding rings seven months
after they married in the First Unitarian Church
in Duluth. Jeff remembers negotiations
to end the Viet Nam War, how months were wasted
trying to choose the right conference table.

Jerry finds that the rings change. His sucks
clouds from treetops, rolls them around like gumballs.
Jeff's plays harmonica by the Saint Louis River. Lulling
songs draw mosquitoes and hummingbirds.

Two years into their marriage, a radical way of life
that includes taking the trash out on Monday nights
and mowing the lawn, Jeff looks down on his left hand.
Where's the ring? He and Jerry search the house.
No luck.

They find it under the refrigerator. Minerva the cat
had probably batted it underneath. They wouldn't
have found it except they had to get the ice maker fixed
so it had to be moved out from the wall.

By now, the harmonica player has moved on.
Even the robins and mosquitoes have flown off.
Years stack up, bubble-glass plates
about to tip over, others like orchids blooming
when winter carries an axe to the house.

Door Locked

Jeff and his work buddies
head to Bob's Tap
after work. They all know Jeff
is married to Jerry. They're cool
with it but sometimes . . .

Carl says, I'm trying remember
a song title from, I think, *Cats*,
Jeff, you'd know it,
you guys love show tunes. Jeff,
more Led Zeppelin and Joan Jett,
orders another pitcher, talks about
the Brewers—another closet
Jeff wants to pop out of.
A Yankees fan, he starts his day
with sports scores, takes it personally
when they lose. Closets,

he thinks, get so deep
that one leads to another.
You wander,
door locked.

Jerry Home

The sky changes like sherry
when you add
an ice cube.

We run after bundled
packages
of reality
tossed in a trash truck,
watch as it turns a corner
and disappears.

Gunfire Buddha

Jeff put a statue of Buddha
on top of the freezer. Buddha looks

happy despite a wet cat litter smell.
Jeff mostly avoids religion,
makes an exception for Buddha,
full of mountains and lotuses.
Jerry would "like" Buddha on Facebook
but would prefer him placed elsewhere—
the freezer top already holds eight
rolls of paper towels, three batteries,
five novena candles, and one vase
that looks uglier each year but
Jeff's grandmother willed it to him.
Maybe Buddha

blesses where a gum pop
could be gunfire.

Jerry Says

to Jeff: I can't
compare you to a summer's day
since you hate summer,
except for the fishing,
and you prefer night. I can

compare you to little. Sometimes
you're like a swimming pool.
I jump in. The water
takes me in. Or,
drained, maple leaves
scudding on the bottom,
nothing to jump in to.

We're winter spirits.
Between us, a snowflake falls.
Call it a kiss. We dream spring,
believe in it
like we believe in God,
a tigridia bloom's magenta
heaven declaring war
on brevity. No more comparisons.

Be. Set similes free.
Summer, winter. The calendar
cuts it up and serves.

Jeff and Jerry on Separate Vacations

Jeff flies to Las Vegas. Desert
ice sculptures thrive like cacti.

Jerry visits Madeline Island, which
publishes a newspaper made of snow,
builds a house from icicles. Back home,

when Jeff goes to Randy's Sports Bar,
Jeff slips into bed and a book
on Tudor England, loves peace
and heads rolling.

Next year they'll travel together,
seeking a moment when,
in a row boat, the sun
frog leaps under a lily pad.

Jeff and Jerry with the Travel Agent

They agree to go somewhere
vastly different from Oshkosh.
Once they arrive, they can tear up
identities like used tickets.

Jerry says that if he were a cat
with nine lives, one would be
a flat-out time-wasting, crumply bum.
Jeff says he'd shimmy up to pick
coconuts though he dislikes their taste—
how fun to challenge a tree,
a large knife downing a cluster.

The travel agent heaps up options.
After two hours they decide
not to decide. Probably another

summer spent lugging home
soil bags from Lowe's, getting
both cars inspected, inertia
like a humid night on the porch,
no one talking.

Jerry and Jeff in Cape May

The sun gobbles up the horizon line,
sets a cellophane sky on fire.
It's romantic.

Jerry says "Oh, Jeff"
and Jeff says there's a great
restaurant a mile away.
They stay in a refurbished
Victorian house, Jerry's idea
of bliss. Jeff would be fine
with a Motel Six. Sex,

finding a sheltered place
when rain pours down—
you get to see the sun pop
back out, blankets cover wet sand,
the ocean
laced with light.

Jerry and Jeff at the International Peace Garden

A garden from 1932.
150,000 flowers planted
every summer. Peace
ought to bloom loudly
in this quiet.

Many people right now
would kill Jeff and me
for being gay.

If they kill us here,
our graves will have
flowers aplenty.
We hold hands. Joy
sounds mournful
like a lake loon.

We wait for that sound.
We count on it.

Missing Each Other

Jerry slops around in sweatpants
and a tee. Jeff fishes in Wisconsin
by himself, a trip he makes

once a year despite mosquitoes.
Jerry uses their parting for movies.
He's already watched

eight Barbara Stanwyck films,
topping them off with *Double
Indemnity*. Now it's time for

*The Kingfisher Illustrated
Horse & Pony Encyclopedia*,
not that he likes horses much,

but any encyclopedia is a salmon
dahlia almost open when
you're alone. He learns

how to soak a haynet, what exercises
to do in the saddle. He's never
even been on a pony. When Jeff returns,

Jerry will explain the ways
of horses. Jeff will harrumph
that the fish weren't biting,

a conversation speeding
in opposite directions,
canter and bait.

Jeff, Jerry, & the Lap

Jerry says, "The chance of winning the lottery
is one in a billion. Decent odds!"
Jeff buys tickets, displays them on the mantle.
They both pray, believing
there's a one in a billion chance
that God hears or cares,

but why not? Lightning hit Jerry's Aunt Lu
while she talked on the phone.
Strange things happen—
once they do they're less strange.

Jeff pines to sit on the lap of luxury,
fate stroking his head like a cat.
He pictures Jerry and himself
swimming in a gold ocean. They get off the lap,

go to work, settle for crumb cake
and a K-Mart going out of business sale.

Caps

Jerry shouts that Jeff shouldn't screw
caps on bottles so tight. Jeff says
it keeps fizz in. This escalates.

The sun puts an ear
to the door and hears all
the juicy stuff—only mildly juicy.

Besides, they know the sun's secrets,
including that affair the sun had
with a hot star in Andromeda. Junk
gets out eventually. At dusk
Jeff and Jerry watch a reddening sky
rouge the yard. Dahlias look made up—

petals wink when the wind walks by.

Jerry Listening to the Wind

Wind had only one hit,
"Make Believe." Most of
high school was make believe—

smiling for bullies, smiling
for Pastor, or smiling for teachers
who fed us poisoned algebra.
It turns out that Wind
was only studio musicians—
how could there be no Wind?

I waited for a good strong one
to blow through my school.
It never came.

Just a stillness
I didn't dare break
by speaking.

Mosquito Jeff

Jeff hangs rosary beads
around his rear
view mirror. Just in case.

Last May he tried to pass
a semi, almost hit a Kia head on.
Beads wiggled and wobbled.
He remembers other close calls,
the first in second grade
when a tall cabinet fell,
pinning him to the floor.

Death, his worst enemy,
best friend. Either way,
he's followed. Footsteps
make him think he's cornered
even when a falling oak
leaf is the day's biggest event.
He listens—something's trying

to catch him, a mosquito,
in its bare hand.

Jeff and Jerry have Ants

Jeff smashes them between his fingers.
Even as a boy he'd hose down
their colonies, a pretend game

of Flood. Jerry prefers lightly
sweeping them onto a cake plate
and putting them outdoors.
Who are they hurting? Why kill
when they're only guilty of
coming inside—they enter
as if invited. When Jeff pinches

another one to death,
Jerry winces, begins to side
with the ants almost.
Jeff is usually gentle.
When Jerry had pneumonia, Jeff
fed him soup and fluffed his pillows.
He joined EarthJustice. Jerry

wonders if his own cruelty hides
under one of his ribs
ready to spring loose. He can
say things that wound for years.
The ants,

feisty little things,
carry a sugar crumb
across a kitchen floor's desert.

In Jerry's Dream

Jeff takes him
to Rio. A samba starts
when they get to the beach,
Sugarloaf Mountain sipping
a Quentao in a cloud. They dance
even though in real
life they do that poorly. Here
a soft percussive beat rises
up from their feet, pulses
through their bodies.

The scene changes. It's the Yukon.
In January. The thermometer prays
to a god it doesn't believe in
for just one warm degree.
Jeff and Jerry huddle, sure
they won't outlive the night,

but they do—woodpeckers
at the suet feeder, the coffeemaker's
light wheeze, Brazil and Yukon
with tails high, hungry.

Block Party

1.

325 Oak Street talks with 318 Oak Street. Marsha says, "I had to invite the gay ones. It would look unfriendly if I didn't."

Belle says, "I just hope they don't, you know, start kissing or something. Jack would probably get a gun or something."

"Or something."

Both in their forties, Jeff and Jerry live at 345 Oak Street. Yesterday, after Jeff got home from his job at Home Depot, he husked corn while Jerry put push pins through the porch screen which flops down whenever there's wind. From there it's a quick leap to gay marriage, gay adoption, and the fall of the Western world.

Speaking of the fall, it's early October. A breeze lifts a few paper plates off the table set in the middle of Oak Street which has been blocked off for the annual block party. Lemonade sweats in a ruby pitcher. Hamburger patties, red as faces of sprinting runners, sit under a thin plastic wrap.

Speaking of the fall. Of Western Civilization. It happens all the time. Western Civilization, nicknamed Wes, attends the block party too. He sits on a thatched chaise lounge, sips a margarita, with salt, and moans to Belle about diabetes and why it's so hard to put together a gas grill. I mean, the box says, "4 Easy Steps" and you get in it and a billion widgets and whatsits fall out. Honestly.

Marsha offers corn chips and salsa.

"Care for some chips, Wes?"

"No thanks, honey. I'm on a diet."

Marsha breezes off—her kid Rodney knocked over the chocolate cake with vanilla icing she had made.

"Damn you, Rodney!"

The boy escapes over a hedge.

Rodney can't stand his parents, especially his dad Charles, nicknamed Chuck, who smokes and his beer belly looks like a row boat on a choppy lake. Wes likes Rodney, calls him a "scamp," and thinks Marsha and Charles are the salt of the Earth, licking the edge of his grita glass. He avoids Cara, the adopted five-year-old daughter of Maxine and Lila, 355 Oak, won't even talk to her, just slumps in his chaise. A speed demon in his youth, friends called him "lead foot," but that was long ago. Now his knees ache and it's hard just to get up to go to the bathroom.

2.

After stuffing themselves on dogs and burgers, Jeff and Jerry say goodbye and head back to 345. Maxine, Lila, and Cara join them. Jeff and Jerry don't like kids, but Cara is "cute," at least that's what Jeff says. Jerry considers kids to be tiresome interferences in adult conversation. Maxine laughs like Tallulah Bankhead. Lila likes colorful hats with broad brims.

"That Marsha," says Lila, "her grande-dame at forty bit is getting old. You could peel her smile off in layers, like mummy bandages."

"She's alright," says Jeff, "but so nervous. I don't know about what. She seems to have it all."

"And that old guy, Wes, why does he have to come to these parties?" Maxine asks.

"I know, he's a fossil, but Marsha wants to include everyone."

"Did anyone ever like him?" Jeff asks.

"Yeah," Lila says, "he was married once. To a beautiful woman, so I hear, named Felicia, but Felicia got bored and skidaddled all the way to Argentina. I saw a picture of Wes when he was young. Belle says he was some kind of Adonis. Who knew?"

Dusk. A pair of pink flip-flops walking between clouds. A slapping sound of hand on leg from mosquitoes.

Jerry says, "Wes sounds like a pretty sad guy. Jeff, maybe we should have him over for martinis. I know he hates gays, but you never know. Maybe he'll come around. So what if he's thousands of years old?

3.

Jeff: "You always..."

Jerry: "I never!"

Jerry enjoys parties, Jeff doesn't, and living room walls don't dare to take sides. It's the evening they've waited for—Wes has finally agreed to stop in for drinks. Jeff sees him walking up the driveway. Jerry and Jeff have been cleaning all week. Everything has to *sparkle*. That's what Jeff says, *sparkle*, summoning up a word his mother used to say every Friday when she'd move all the furniture, even the couch, to get any errant dust fleck. She called herself The Dust Assassin. Jeff and Jerry usually live just to the north of squalor.

But for this one day the house sparkles. Diamonds, and we don't have to tell anyone that they're phonies, glint on the mantle and light through the bay window shows that how even the mother-in-law's green straps shine.

"Hi Wes, how are you? Hope you're well," Jerry says, opening the door.

"Hello," the voice cold, like a fork found under snow.

Jeff brings in chilled martinis, very dry. Wes grabs one, downs it, grabs another. Jerry and Jeff trade glances, laugh, and Wes begins a tirade. Every other sentence starts "I don't like . . ." Jeff tries to change the subject, but the subject never settles.

Jerry fluffs a pillow and just as he's about to bring it to Wes, he slumps.

"Wes! Wes! What's wrong?" asks Jerry while Jeff skitters to the phone.

Too late. When the ambulance arrives, Wes is dead. A heart attack—of course in a queer house. Uh, oh, what will the newspapers say? And worse, what will Marsha say? He declined and fell even before the garlic bagel crisps made it to the coffee table.

Neighbors gather outside of 345 and watch three ambulance guys haul Wes away. Some weep and shake their heads. A cloud. Of suspicion. Hangs. Over 345.

Marsha and the others, like waves receding from a water lily, drift back to their houses. "Heart attack, ha!" Jerry hears Chuck say. Blame's sperm meets Guilt's egg.
A new world forms. And in the morning, the kids must be driven to band practice, haircuts happen, and jobs open their unlipsticked mouths for many on Oak Street to sidle up and kiss.

Don't Talk (Put Your Head on My Shoulder)

Jerry and Jeff argue about
Pet Sounds. Jeff says it's not only
the greatest Beach Boys album,
but the greatest album. Ever. Jerry sniffs,
prefers *Wild Honey--Pet Sounds*
Is like a dog bred for shows.

The house shivers
as they throw insults and accusations.
The louder they get, the more
they realize that they're fighting
over music they agree on.
They each love both albums.

Winded, they sit on the glider,
watch dusk drip into night.
Fireflies make the buddleia look
like a radio station transmitter
hides in blossoms. Don't talk,

says Jeff. Jerry gets quiet,
puts his head on Jeff's shoulder.
The quiet is like a window
that no one can break.
If only for a few hours.

Evening slips away like a needle
finding the run-out groove,
the last song lost in darkness.

Indoor Garden

As winter sprints near their driveway,
Jerry lugs in fuschias, a plumeria,
an abutilon, a waist-high gardenia
for a warm bay window, transfers
a salmon double-flowered Christmas
cactus to the dining room window.

Buds look like people
standing in a crowded elevator,
no hope of the door opening
soon. Snow

makes the window ache.
Color trembles on the sill.

Stung

Jerry unwittingly plants a purple datura
on top of an underground hornet's nest.
Out they come, stinging him
three times. He screams as he runs

to the house—the air conditioner runs
and an open can of fizzy water
(black cherry) goes flat on the counter.
A painting of a hummingbird could use
dusting above the TV
which is now off but later Jeff
will want to watch that Mary Tyler Moore
marathon which they will do since
they both love Mary. Last Christmas's
advent calendar, all days open, still
rests on the mantle beside a red vase
that Jeff got in the hospital thrift shop.
That nice older lady, Harriet Something,
sometimes talks to him about
the Yankees if she's not busy. Jerry
flings open the overstuffed medicine cabinet,
pops a Benadryl, wraps ice
from the ice maker in a towel.
Jeff presses it on his wounds

as Jerry rapidly explains what happened
and he didn't get enough dirt
around the base of the datura
so will it grow strong and bloom
or wither away like that sad
white hollyhock behind the shed.

Magic

Jerry waits for magic,
leaves on the porchlight
in case it should pop

in at night. Jeff does what he can,
but the house still needs cleaning,
the lawn mowing.

Jeff shrugs off magic,
scrambles eggs and if it's sunny
he'll wash the car. Jerry

thinks today the talking goldfish
will appear.
Even for an afternoon,
even for a single minute ringed
with gold and stretching all the way
past the grave.

Rituals

Evening Ritual

Before he turns in, Jerry puts his face on. Jeff is bored. After twenty-three years, he knows every angle of Jerry's face. He blows Jerry a kiss which lands on a watchband. Jerry needs no make-up, blush, eye liner, or lipstick. It's the whole face. He takes out the eyes, worn, with bags beneath, and replaces them with fresh ones, brown not blue. And the mouth, goodbye to that pinched look. Marilyn Monroe could live in this mouth. The receding hairline, in the trash. He musses a full head of hair.

The next day Jerry does this to his soul. He can rearrange whoever he is, remake it with sparkles and onions. A highway with exits to fast-food joints becomes a forest where ferns elect owls to lead a summer choir. Moss gambles with pebbles. A dark forest, fabulous, where a birch tree mambos with only the most sumptuous creek.

The new self fills in quickly. Jerry keeps it to himself, even from Jeff. He sleeps with the window open to hear crickets. Fireflies invite him to a den in mid-air. Their lights are tiny New York City's hovering over purple buddleia blooms. Jerry, at last, is fully himself. A new kind of coming out—to the wind, the shed door's clackety-clap, a skunk brushing up against the bottom of the green garbage can before heading under a shy rhododendron.

Slobs

Walk in their living room,
trip over cat toys, slip
on newspapers. Jeff means to gather
the many Sports sections that pile up.
There's a crossword puzzle to do.
Jerry whines and says "Please
pick up after yourself," sounding like
his mom telling him to clean his room
in seventh grade. Jerry leaves 45s

on each table, Brenda Lee's
"Is It True" stained by coffee.
When they go to bed, the papers
and records don't miss them.
They have orgies and bake sales.
Jeff sometimes dreams of a planet
with not a single rock. Jerry
dreams little. He waits for one
that's so beautiful that it might

kill him. In the morning
the paper boy pitches the paper
against the door. Jeff takes it in.
Jerry puts on the coffee maker,
pulls out a random record.
Bill Anderson. "If You Can Live With It
(I Can Live Without It)." Sun glints
off of the marmalade bowl. A kiss
and two engines running.

Jerry's Luck

You're one of the few
who always has good luck. Shit falls
all over the world and you get an umbrella.
Remember when we went to
that fancy party last year?
I tripped on my tongue and your shoes.
You, of course, looked nonchalant
and gorgeous holding a Triscuit with cheese,
smiling like a monkey wound up
and ready to dance. Compassion?
You blithely go your way,
the happiest strawberry in the fruit bin.

Have we finally found a parking place?
If you were driving, we'd be
parking in the middle of Macy's.
Oh gee, don't get all over-sensitive.
We'll shop. Lighten up.
There's Ruby Tuesdays.
Knowing my luck, it'll be closed.

Wood Blocks

Sometimes Jeff gets furious
from selling Sears appliances—
he comes home and stares
at the walls. Jerry has stopped
Asking, "Can I get you anything?"
Jeff needs a tube of quiet,
nothing more. Sometimes

he walks into the basement,
puts wood blocks in a vise
and saws them wafer thin,
a form of communion
with crickets that sometimes
dart out from behind the dryer.
What to do with fifty or more
thin wood pieces? Use them
for poker chips? They end up

as kindling. He comes upstairs,
hugs Jerry who is busy making
a key lime pie which will flop again.

Jeff is ready to talk about their days,
bits of wood in his collar,
the fire slowly taking off.

The First Fallen Petal

Jerry and Jeff spend
a romantic evening. That means
The Vogues *Moments To Remember* CD
and scentless candles (perfume-y things

make Jerry sneeze). Jeff says
that he wants the world to be
this way all the time. He resents
that Earth keeps turning,
that the sun elbows out
the moon. The phone coughs—
someone down the street has died.

Jerry wants life to be key lime pie
for two. He often eats too much,
making some very unromantic
burps. The Vogues sing about standing
on the corner and watching
all the girls go by. The guys
don't want to stand on a corner

or watch girls. A five-dollar bouquet
of pink roses opens fully
on the dining room table.

It's perfect. In the morning,
the first fallen petal.

Jerry says that being

gay is like going
to Heaven and God gives
you the mansion
right next door
to Judy Garland's—

she'll sing if
you ask her to,
which of course you do,
she stands by the piano,
millions join in,

God joins in too,
a little
offkey.

Cardboard Jeff

When I told my best friend Ted
that I liked guys, he stopped
coming over. I got used
to being the body on
the other side of a slammed door.

Music took me in. A song
was like my grandmother's lap,
comforting and warm. Even

nice kids said, "Just try
being straight,"
as if sexuality was
learning to like carrots.
It's odd to talk

about this. I prefer the past
to be a box In the attic. Sometimes
I see it when I climb up
for wrapping paper. I'd love
to take it down and toss it out.

I can't. The cardboard would break—
too much stuff
would get out.

Jerry Puzzles

Dad kept the *Chicago Tribune*
dated November 22, 1963, yellow
paper like old skin. I'd be born

fifteen years later. Mom said that
America rotted after JFK died.
Dad said it would have been better
had Nixon won. I haven't saved

a single paper. News, a dried-up lake.
I'm a deer bolting onto the road,
scared of any direction. Everything
true and false at the same time.

Dad says count on a gun.
Mom says count on nothing.
She may be right, the way a Sudoku
gets solved if you're logical enough.
I'm not. Puzzles sneak up behind me—
I can't outrun them.

Jeff's Curtains

Jeff thinks of Grandma Kate sitting
alone in a ruby chair at Christmas
talking to herself about Canasta—
few know how to meld anymore.
He seldom gets angry, but
when he does it's curtains.
Jerry eats chips in bed
when Jeff's trying to watch
The Honeymooners. Jerry's
crunching enflames Jeff more.
If Jerry says you look cute
when you're mad

Jeff knows he will blow the bed
up like a helium balloon and watch it
drift over oak trees, letting
Jerry out in empty space.

Jerry Bats

at the many icicles weighing down
old gutters. They crash into pieces,
the sound making him grin
under leafless trees. Jerry lets

the fragments lay, sun glinting
off each one. He could wait
for a warm day to melt them,
but he grabs his gloves and goes out,

saves the biggest for last, the one
hanging beyond the dining room
like an ice tree root. He taps
the shovel against it a few times

until chunks fall where dragon wing
begonias had bloomed, a light
red made of dusk
before autumn set its trap.

Jerry Grew Up Thinking

that America would last forever. He
also thought that M.A.S.H. would never
go off the air. Or Carol Burnett.
Forever, like milk, has a shelf life.

He attended each July Fourth parade
carrying a little flag. In high school
his Holiday Inn boss had him
raise and lower the flag,
wrap it up nicely each dusk. Once,
on a windy day, he let it touch
the ground, prayed for forgiveness
to a God he barely believed in.
Now he wonders if America is
a drug that makes you see movie stars
and games. He remembers when

he got locked in school, lights out,
screaming for help—which did come,
but by then he could only tremble.
He's been trembling ever since.
Not showing it. Not letting his heart
touch the ground. The flag
searching for a pole where
the Holiday Inn looked
a bulldozer in the eye and lost.

Charley Pride Sings

Heart Songs, the album that Jeff
says is his alltime favorite,
even more than Bette Midler's first.

Jeff is feisty about music—
either it's great or it's awful,
and if you like something awful,
you're a ninny. This bugs Jerry

who likes many records
that Jeff considers awful,
has a complete 1910 Fruitgum Co.
collection, sings "Simon Says"
in the shower so that Jeff slams
the bathroom door shut. Sometimes
a music fight spatters them
like bacon grease. About art,

Jeff often sneers. In a museum,
he races through the Van Gogh's
and Rousseau's, preferring art
that replicates reality—
"I get that," he says

to Jerry who has already drifted
into Georgia O'Keeffe's "Clouds."
Jerry says, "She puts me there." Jeff
keeps his feet on the ground, a steel
guitar as perfect to him
as Pollack's tipped over paint cans
are to Jerry.

Robber

Jerry hunts down
Chicago-area tunes from 50 years ago,
wants every single released
on the Destination label.

Jeff loves records too,
but he buys glass—
Depression-era glass,
Rob and Laura Petrie's living room glass,
cranberry glass. The house

is breakable. They know
they must cut back. Jerry misses
clean surfaces. Jeff dreams
of a bulldozer shoving it all
out the door. Collecting,

a fever lasting for decades,
a cold that never lets go. Sometimes
they're afraid to have people over.
Stuff,

even fun stuff, is like a robber
who takes your space—
you never get it back.
He breaks in.
You pour him a beer.

Cracked Windowbox

Jerry watches a *Beverly Hillbillies* rerun—
Granny and Mrs. Drysdale at odds.
Jeff rearranges garage crap

he can't bear to get rid of.
Nancy Sinatra drops by in go-go boots
that have walked to several galaxies

since the 60s. The three drink lemonade
poured from a cranberry-red pitcher.
Whitman pops in when Nancy leaves,

his weathervane beard pointing
to heaven and a bowling alley.
Night bubbles on the roof,

black oatmeal. Jerry and Jeff think
that tomorrow may bring a letter
from God, everything fully explained

in simple language. For right now,
they blow a kiss to a trembling fuchsia
reddening a cracked window box.

Jeff and Jerry Up

In a hot air balloon, they float
over farms and groves, land
a disappearing puzzle piece. Up
they go, only Jerry finds that he
has acrophobia. Jeff says relax.
Jerry remembers his friend Marsha
who got him up on the ferris wheel—
it stopped. She rocked it fiercely.
Jerry puked.

All he wants is ground
that petunias clutch,
dew on his feet,
a cloud's tall white hat
as he bends to weed.

Jerry and Jeff don't believe in

an afterlife even though it cries
in a playpen near the broom closet.
They don't hear it—
or see the playpen. Neighbors
hear the crying. They knock and say,
"Stop that baby from crying!"

What crying? A week ago
the afterlife broke out
and crawled into bed with them.
Jeff growled, "Mitsy, you bad cat!"
Jerry turned over--another bad dream.

In the morning they banged
into the playpen, not even an ouch
for a stubbed toe, turned on
another game show
where people who will soon be dead
win wonderful prizes.

10:45 PM

Jeff and Jerry sit on the couch
after a long day. Silence,
beautiful in its way, like a glass
filled with artificial snow, shaken.

Or a horse that lies down in a field.

Some days it's best to send words out to play,
the world slipping
into pajamas and going to sleep.

About the Author

Kenneth Pobo is the author of twenty-one chapbooks and nine full-length collections. Recent books include *Bend of Quiet* (Blue Light Press), *Loplop in a Red City* (Circling Rivers), *Dindi Expecting Snow* (Duck Lake Books), *Wingbuds* (cyberwit.net), and *Uneven Steven* (Assure Press). *Opening* is forthcoming from Rectos Y Versos Editions.

Human rights issues, especially as they relate to the LGBTQIA+ community, are a constant presence in his work. In addition to poetry, he writes fiction and essays. For the past thirty-plus years he taught at Widener University. He retired in 2020.

Thanks to the Editors of the following magazines and presses for publishing these works:

"Jeff And Jerry Were Older" *Bacopa*

"Migrations" *Shantih*

"Jeff And Jerry And The Everyday" *Weatherbeaten Lit*

"Cabinets" *The Bear*

"Jeff And Jerry Wake Up One Saturday" *Writers Against Prejudice*

"Jeff Sees His Old Church Is Now A CVS" *ArLiJo* (Arlington Literary Journal)

"Jeff Knew" *Razorhouse Magazine*

"Jerry Knew" *Razorhouse Magazine*

"Brown Cords" *ArLiJo* (Arlington Literary Journal)

"Page 234" *The Curious Element*

"Jerry And Maxine" *Toho Journal*

"Jerry's Life" *Philadelphia Stories; Stripped* (PS Books)

"Jerry Coming Out To Mom Twice" *Razorhouse Magazine*

"Breakable" *Verse-Virtual*

"Gunfire Buddha" *Skink Beat*

"Jerry Says" *Verse-Virtual*

"Jeff And Jerry On Separate Vacations" *Weatherbeaten.lit*

"Jerry And Jeff In Cape May" *Razorhouse Magazine*

"Jerry And Jeff At The International Peace Garden" *K'in*

"Missing Each Other" *The Impressment Gang* (Canada)

"Jeff, Jerry, & The Lap" *Empty Mirror*

"Caps" *Verse-Virtual*

"Jerry Listening To The Wind" *Razorhouse Magazine*

"Jeff And Jerry Have Ants" *Vanilla Sex*

"In Jerry's Dream" *Minor Literature(s)*

"Block Party" *Gay Flash Fiction*

"Don't Talk" *Citylit Press: Poet Sounds*

"Indoor Garden" *Toasted Cheese*

"Stung" *Nixes Mate*

"Magic" *The Lake (England)*

"Evening Ritual" *Sweater Weather*

"Slobs" *Backchannels*

"Wood Blocks" *Pittsburgh Poetry Review*

"The First Fallen Petal" *Love Poem Anthology*

"Jerry Says That Being" *Weatherbeaten.lit*

"Cardboard Jeff" *Citron Review*

"Jerry Bats" *Route Seven Review*

"Jerry Grew Up Thinking" *Connecticut River Review*

"Charley Pride Sings" *Verse-Virtual*

"Robber" *Drunk Monkeys*

"Cracked Windowbox" *Mush/Mum*

"Jerry and Jeff Don't Believe In" *Tulsa Review*

Meadowlark POETRY

Books are a way to explore, connect, and discover. Poetry incites us to observe and think in new ways, bridging our understanding of the world with our artistic need to interact with, shape, and share it with others.

Publishing poetry is our way of saying—

> *We love these words,*
> *we want to preserve them,*
> *we want to play a role in sharing them*
> *with the world.*

www.birdypoetryprize.com

Meadowlark Press created The Birdy Poetry Prize to celebrate the voices of our era. Cash prize, publication, and 50 copies awarded annually.

The Birdy is an annual competition.

Final Deadline for Entries: December 1, midnight.

Entry Fee: $25

All entries will be considered for standard Meadowlark Press publishing contract offers, as well.

Full-length poetry manuscripts (55 page minimum) will be considered. Poems may be previously published in journals and/or anthologies, but not in full-length, single-author volumes. All poets are eligible to enter, regardless of publishing history.

See www.birdypoetryprize.com for complete submission guidelines. Also visit us at meadowlark-books.com.

www.ingramcontent.com/pod-product-compliance
Lightning Source LLC
Chambersburg PA
CBHW021450070526
44577CB00002B/348